Tangled

I0192818

Threads

This book is dedicated to Lois Kamp,
one of our poets who died in 2024.
We will miss her forever.

Tangled

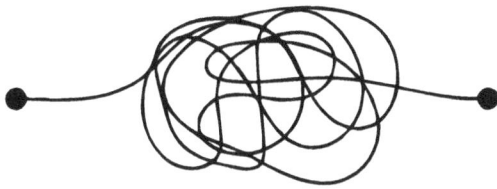

Threads

AN ANTHOLOGY OF THE FIRST FRIDAY POETS

Foreword

This anthology has its once upon a time back in the 1980s. Pam O'Brien was a young mom with three small children and no time to write the poetry she had loved to write in college. Actually, no time to do much of anything creative. She heard from a friend of a friend about a poetry workshop near Lake Chautauqua, New York, and found a way to attend the monthly Saturday meetings. Nancy Whitelaw facilitated this group and prepared Spicy West African Stew for lunch. After sharing stories from their lives while slurping stew, the group held a workshop that involved learning about poetry as well as critiquing each others' poems. People came from as far away as the Finger Lakes and Erie, PA, to attend.

Fast forward to the after-Covid days. O'Brien had retired from the University of Pittsburgh to The Villages, FL. She remembered the Salisbury Hill Poets days of being nurtured, cared for, given space to write her stories. She wanted to replicate Nancy's workshop in a very different setting with a very different age group. She found ten women willing to give it a try. They named the workshop First Fridays. They loved the Spicy West African Stew, the sharing of their lives over lunch, and then the workshop, with a focus on learning about poetry and telling family stories. They loved that someone cooked for them and they encouraged each other creatively.

Some of them had never written a poem. Some were published poets. One was a singer, two were fabric artists, several painted and wrote fiction or devotionals or memoirs. Previously, they had been editors, therapists, teachers, nurses, counselors, columnists, tech writers, and missionaries. They had stayed single or raised families. They had lost spouses and other loved ones.

If this book aims to do one thing, besides encouraging other people to write those memories, it is to encourage those same people to gather in small groups to share food, to talk about their lives, to share both their treasures and their secrets.

Welcome to the work of the First Friday Poets.

Contents

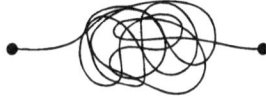

Lorraine Benjamin

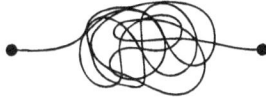

L orraine has been creating since she was a young girl. She describes herself as "a maker." As a child, she would while away hours with needle work and writing story books. She began writing poetry as a teenager and explored this avenue of self-expression until 1997 when she focused her energy on developing her skills as a textile artist.

Her contemporary approach to the needle arts, with its exploration of color, repetition, design, and texture, allowed Lorraine to develop her unique artistic voice. Her creative roots are firmly embedded in the traditional needle arts and this is reflected in her body of work. She began to write poetry again after her retirement in 2022. She frequently pairs the poems that she writes with her visual artwork. Both her poetry and visual art are inspired by her faith, family stories, travels, and the natural world.

Since 1993, Lorraine had lived in the Ithaca area of the Finger Lakes Region in New York. In 2019, she relocated to central Florida. She recently retired from a career in nursing. She enjoys the support of her husband, their children, and grandchildren.

Lorraine is an exhibiting artist and has won several awards for her fiber art.

She owns and operates The Tangled Thread, a longarm quilting business, gives presentations, and teaches classes focused on mixed media and stitched art. She also enjoys acrylic and watercolor painting.

Down On the Farm

The black and white photo
now tattered and worn
taken by my dad in 1960
at the Labor Day picnic
down on the farm.

Sheltered beneath the arms of the great elm tree
one decade before Dutch elm disease,
we stood,
my mother and I.

For her, a rare moment of contentment.
For me, a lesson in familiarity.
She, holding my chubby body
smelling the sweet sweat of late summer tangled in my hair.

Crisp white tablecloths rustled in the breeze,
anchored in place by plates and bowls
heaped with the season's bounty.
The muffled spurts of conversation
spoken between mouthfuls of potato salad and biscuits.
Uncle Gene, his face brown and weathered, asks
"How many heifers you expect will freshen this year?"
Uncle Hinkle grinning, "Hoping for a dozen."

Was she hiding behind me?
Or perhaps displaying me with satisfaction
to this family who measured blessings
in healthy, obedient children?

A contest, it seems, she had won.

My mother, the outsider,
the city girl,
at ease with fashion,
high style,
smart clothes and
Estee Lauder makeup.

Now married to this county boy turned chemist,
first ever to go to college in his family.
Pleased by the acceptance,
this kind family had bestowed upon her,
simply for being Charles' wife
and my mother.

Her slender figure not betraying
she had given birth to her third child
just ten months prior.
She stands there
with her raven-colored hair
and sculptured brows,
her appearance so unlike the ample farm girls.

Did she breathe in the fresh country air,
feel herself relax into its honesty?
Allow herself to be engulfed by its grace?

Pretension slips away
down on the farm.

Overnight at Grandma's

My grandma's old Singer
heavily varnished,
its solid oak "Coffin" cover
my makeshift seat.

My little-girl legs
stretching taut in anticipation,
perched on the edge
tippy toes blindly reaching
barely touching
the hard metal form,
the treadle.

Tasked with pumping
the rhythmic beat
that raises and lowers the needle—
Grandma's hands
expertly guiding mine
as I stitch my first-ever seams.

All those hours spent in stitching
corsets and slips,
repairs by the armful.
I played with the scraps,
while she tended dinner.

Touching texture, watching color,
seeing art for the first time.

Standing in the Silence

Between the lines
a thousand creeds laid bare.

The child of the unseen light
dances a monument
before the sky.

Love easily.

Meet me in the silence
of my yesterdays.
 In dense stillness,
compose me a rhapsody,
nurture my unkempt soul.

Compel me now to trust again.
Lay aside this treason.
Resurrect my devout heart.

The Ancestress

In the belly of sweet longing
remnants kin to Celtic lore
of resistance
of rebellion
brave young maidens of the moor.

Underfoot they crush the thistle
bowed and bloodied, banter stored
find resilience
find redemption
life is battle at its core.

This Arduous Calling

The shrill ring—
then a voice steeped with dank authority
crashes through my tranquil sleep.
I grasp for comprehension
"Collect your grandchildren,"
"Foster Care," "Placement."
Oh yes, these, I fear—
this I understand.
Into the night I rush
towards the dismal flat, now ablaze,
that they called home.

I see her sitting on the sofa,
epic flower child —
my daughter from another mother
costumed in feathers—
tutus and frills,
dripping with
celestial scents of
lavender, eucalyptus
and weed.
My son nowhere to be found.

My nostrils burn with acrid smoke,
the fog-like haze alters my vision —
squinting I glimpse my grandson, Zaide,
still a babe in arms,
and his sister Maddy,
at tempestuous two.

My heart is full.
Of love.
Of pity.
Of terror.
For these my fledgling offspring,
coming home with me.
Sleepless nights,
hectic days,
endless bedtime routines.
Impatience drills into my soul
like an insect into cemented earth.

The upheaval of my ambitions.
But also, a stolen moment—
pure joy.
They call me "Nana-Momma."

This arduous calling.

Elsie Bowman

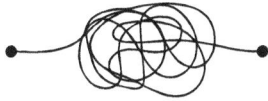

From her earliest years Elsie loved words, the sounds, the sense, even the silliness of words. Much later she learned to recreate her inner world and sometimes her outer world with language.

Her innate shyness and sensitivity and her experience of not being heard as a child led her to be reticent to express her thoughts and feelings out loud in the presence of more than a person or two. That same diffidence kept her from making her written work available to unknown audiences.

Since college, she has shared her writing only with her personal journals and her Word Weavers group. She is forever grateful to Pam O'Brien and her First Friday friends for encouraging her to write more poetry and to find her own voice.

With the help of Pam's instruction and the group support, two recent poems have won first place awards in the Royal Palm and Tapestry contests. Thanks to Pam and Jack O'Brien we will see our poems published, some of us for the first time. Praise the Lord!

A psychotherapist by vocation, Ms. Bowman's life has been blessed by her beloved husband, daughter, son, stepson, five grandchildren and wonderful friends.

Solace of Summer Songs

In the early years, summer sang to me.
Then, hours lingered, languid and liquid.
Then, days lazed along a lonesome river.

Her arms parched and peeled, pomegranate-pink
her hair salty and stringy as seaweed
her face sticky-sweet, watermelon-wet.

She swam light as leaves in the deepest seas.
She ran in rhythm with the welcome rain.
She sailed off a swing into the bright sun.

Then, a diamond hid in every rock.
A firefly scribed secret messages.
A raindrop displayed a thousand splendors.

In the early years
Time rocked me gently
safe in a hammock
made of holy hands.

Autumn Leaving on a Freight Train

In the middle years, autumn allured me
and alarmed me. Then, each day dazzled with
delights while a wild river propelled me.

Turn off alarm hit floor splash face grab clothes
wake up kids make coffee wake kids again
make lunches find shoes find keys jump in car.

A fire blazed brightly from dawn to night.
Blessings brimmed over the best-kept baskets.
Burdens stacked up like bulky bales of hay.

Fight traffic find parking place return calls
answer emails help clients make meetings
write reports fill out forms play politics.

The sun glowed golden in the blue-grey skies.
Purple and rust and yellow splashed the trees.
Cinnamon and cider scented the house.

Cook dinner wash dishes wash clothes pay bills
buy groceries change the oil wash the dog
mow the lawn visit family volunteer.

In the middle years, the freight train of time
pursued me with relentless speed, spitting
fumes that mingled with the fragrance of fall.

Whispered Wings of Winter

In the last years, winter wrapped her in white
as snow settled, soft, silent, still, and steep,
but a new spring burst forth from the cold earth.

Then, the first crocus made her spirit soar.
A robin's song invited her to dance.
The pink dawn painted her heart in rainbows.

The hours let go like day-old petals
but each moment held promise of a pearl
and, with time, trust triumphed over trying.

She steadied her steps and forged a straight path.
She found a place of peace and purpose.
She became the prayer whispered at her birth.

In the last years, she floated on whispers
of white wings, carefree as a cloud, so high
she beheld the face of her beloved.

Like Grass That Grows

Grass lavishes in lawns of landowners
and stampedes in the yards of the struggling.
It congregates in the common country
and sends out its spies to the city streets.

Sea grass survives on the shores' shifting sands.
Rye grass rises ruglike on forest floors.
Pampas grass hitchhikes in the desert.
Windmill grass winds around the roughest rocks.

Like grass that grows green and gratuitous
God's grace finds its way to meet every need.

On the days when all windows open wide
on the nights when darkness closes all doors
in the clamor and chaos of the crowds
in the still silence of solitude

when the seas of sorrow overwhelm me
when the forest of fears blinds my vision
when my dreams disappear like a mirage
when I cannot scale up one more steep step

Then God's grace sprouts up all around me
like a green pasture to restore my soul.

Sunsets and Passing Parades

The setting sun does not really set.
Our world turns and tilts until
 daylight departs and night encloses.

But sometimes the sky brings surprises
with corals of pink and peach
that burst alive from the deep blue seas.

Or with molten gold that melts and glows
on streams of crimson copper
that flow from a pool of platinum.

Or a songful of glossy starlings
and a purple martin flock
followed by flamboyant flamingos.

Then our heavy burdens fall away
as we are captivated
by a glimpse of beauty and beyond.

So too when my last parade has passed
may ribbons of remembrance
lighten hearts and turn eyes toward Heaven.

Robin Collison

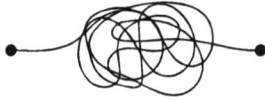

A ward winning author Robin Collison earned her first writing prize at seventeen, winning first place—lunch with then-Poet Laureate Carl Sandburg—in a nation-wide poetry contest. After graduating as valedictorian of the University of Maryland, she became a movie critic for seven coast-to-coast newspapers. Robin copyrighted 102 self-improvement seminars during 40 years as director of a charitable nonprofit.

Other work includes: a story in the Australian anthology *Forgiveness is the Hardest Thing* (2022); *The Fine Art Club of Shrimpboat Key* (WIP four-book series about child artists overcoming barriers to success, four pre-publication awards); *The Listener of Morpho Island* (WIP Dystopian trilogy, three pre-publication awards); *Maximize Your Health/Get Your Life on Track*, a *Guide for Life-Altering Disabilities*, and *Kaleidoscope*, an early collection of poetry.

Robin sings in state parks to entertain campers, edits the books of young novelists, jogs two hours a day, and serves as President of the Ocala Writing Coaches group.

The Banshee Wraith of Whyatt, Illinois

(Heaven and Earth)
       Part One: In Heaven

"Are you ready to go to Heaven?"
Grandma Charylin tugged the frayed cord.
The ceiling creaked open, showered us with sawdust.
I held my breath. Covered my face as
       the ladder descended
with an eerie whistle, like a ghost train.

We climbed steep stairs with a shaky handrail.
In the gloom, dusty yearbooks formed a messy stack,
a steamer trunk displayed crumbled stickers from Spain,
a dressmaker's dummy wore a
       mildewed wedding gown.
Dark corners held cobwebs no broom could sway.

I clutched my body in a self-hug, trembled as
a black widow spider eyed me from her web.
The prairie wind moaned through cracks in the boards.
"She still lives up here," Grandma pointed at
       a human skull,
"Rosheen's mother, the Banshee Wraith of Whyatt."

I shrank back, too scared to speak,
 skedaddled from this Heaven
filled with decomposing memories.
Fled down the ladder, hid beneath the
       crazy quilt
stitched by the woman whose spirit prowled the attic.

Part Two: On Earth

After the fried chicken and corn-on-the-cob,
after the strawberry shortcake and lemonade,
Great-grandmother Rosheen Whyatt strode home
from the park, balancing the family canoe
        on her head,
lake water dripping into her fire-red hair.

That night, she pulled on her homemade white nightgown,
spied the teardrop diamond ring of her Banshee mother
(nicknamed for keening at sick beds) missing from her finger.
We searched the house and porch, canoe, picnic hamper.
        Stress mounted
like the Shamrock ivy on the back porch lattice.

Hours later, a white wraith slipped out the side door of
102 East Jackson Street, glided down the porch steps,
past stumps of trees felled by Dutch elm disease.
The apparition floated the tar-and-pebble road to Lake Whyatt.
        Sightless eyes
regarded the Whyatt Oak, picnic tables, and monkey bars, searching.

Rosheen woke with the glittery ring on her finger,
but no memory of how it got there.
Did she sleepwalk to the park, find it herself?
Or did her Banshee mother climb down from Heaven to
        retrieve her own diamond?
Two generations later, we still get goosebumps when we tell the tale.

The Day the Duckling Drowned

The big-nosed stranger in the soldier's uniform
tosses me high in the air,
catches me in strong arms.
      "You're awfully small for a five-year-old."

I take giant steps
like when we play "Mother May I,"
but he tugs my arm to rush me.
      "Hurry up, we're going on an adventure."

"What's an adventure?"
The stranger who calls himself Daddy looks down.
"Well, I guess it's something you've
      never done before.

"Now skip down the hill to the duck pond
while I make a movie with my camera."
Oh, a camera. Grandma Charylin taught me to
      curtsy for the camera.

Two feet from the duckpond,
I search for fluffy baby ducks.
Last week they let me pat them, then scurried back
to their mom for safety.

I reach to touch a mushroom.
Oops, five muddy fingers.
I wipe them in the grass. *Mommy hates it when*
      I come home dirty.

Stranger Daddy raises his voice, gestures with one hand.
"Move back near the water. Good, a little more."
Trusting him with the faith of a child,
        I step back.

The movie shows a tiny girl
beam a smile and curtsy,
then plunge backward into the pond
        and vanish from sight.

It's a silent film, but you almost hear the splash.
Ducks paddle for their lives, goldfish dart
to the opposite shore. I flap my arms in panic.
        You almost hear the scream.

I hit the water hard.
My breath puffs out in a rush.
Bullrushes tangle around my feet,
        dragging me down.

The camera rises to the trees,
then plummets down, filming
the fingers of a drowning child
        grasping handfuls of air

while the stranger in the starched uniform
plunges into waist-deep water
to haul her out.
        You almost hear him curse.

Stranger Daddy wrings out his shirt
and lays it across a wild blackberry bush.
He tries to cheer me up while the sun dries
  my dripping red checkered dress.

"Do you want to roll down the hill?"
I do not want to roll down the hill.
I choke on pond foam,
  unable to answer.

"Do you want a strawberry ice cream cone?"
My wet hair drips onto my knees,
filling my patent leather church shoes
  with smelly water.

"Reach into your pocket. Maybe you caught a goldfish."
I do not want to find a goldfish.
My sodden dress clings to my legs
  and I need to pee.

Yesterday the outside world was harmless.
Now my trust lies drowned in the mud
of the duckpond. I want to scurry back
  to Mommy for safety.

Coeds on the sidewalk glare at the Stranger-Daddy.
"She's shaking with cold, mister."
"Better take her home."
  I smother a sob, wondering,
  if I can't trust my daddy, who can I trust?

My Panther Lover, 1968

(First Impression)
The man with the horn has inscrutable intentions.
He glares at the crowd then leaps onstage
with a crashing chord and a guttural growl,
trailing generations of onyx ancestors
     like a pied patchwork cape.

The man with the horn is cloaked with flimflam.
His pensive puma eyes disguise
centuries-old fury. His skin traces a
tangle of scars from his forebears' miseries
     as the Massa's flayed prey.

(Second Impression)
Each night you stalk onto the boards
seeking subtly to even old scores.
Your shrewd scornful lyrics
punish fans for prattling
     like pompous entitled knaves.

My love is tinged with generational guilt,
yours, with the quest for righteous revenge.
Under my granny's patchwork quilt,
it gets crowded as lavish liberals
     wrestle with sullen slaves.

Dialogue with an Old Friend
at Age Forty-Eight

I lost my power serve one bright June morning,
woke up that Tuesday and it was gone,
slunk away overnight like an out-of-sorts lover.
My best friend Kay cut me no slack
pounding returns with effortless whacks.

      Never again to score on my first serve?
      I could live with that.

A year later I lost my cartwheel.
I, who turned double back flips and lined
my parent's mantel with gymnastics trophies.
"Did you forget how?" my children asked winking.
They were airborne while I was sinking.

      Never again to show off on the beach?
      I could live with that.

But when Beauty began to melt away like the snow
on Mt. Kilimanjaro, leaving bare
basalt where once shone
dazzling panoramas, I plummeted downslope.
Sweet fashionista, by God, I'm gonna miss ya.

It was Beauty, not Kay, who coached me to shorten hemlines,
Beauty, not Kay, who coaxed me to ignore brassiere guidelines.

Beauty, you've been my sister, my soulmate,
my cheerleader, secret keeper, door opener,
reputation, inspiration, liberation,
magician, tactician, physician,
my ace in the hole at dance competitions.

At a 1966 pageant, I accepted an armful
of long-stemmed American Beauty roses.
My stems are now short and bulbous. My bloom has died.
No tears can revive my turgor.
I fear I might have the blight.

      Never again to hear a wolf whistle?
      I guess I could live with that.

Brown spots embroider my legs,
Skin cancer scars lace my face,
my hair's no longer Bonfire Red.
On the dance floor I'm a slow two-stepper
with locks piled in buns salt-and-pepper.

I still rush to the mirror each morning hoping
it has snowed on Mt. Kilimanjaro.
Tears sting when my BFF Beauty
once again fails to show up
for our tennis date.

      Never again to see Miss America in the mirror?
      Can I live with that?

Take my right arm, take my digestion,
take my mobility if you must.
But don't take away my best friend.
I've leaned on Beauty since I was four months old.
I'm not sure I can hike this mountain alone.

Youth melts off my face,
drips from sagging breasts,
runs down varicosed legs,
puddles beneath rough feet.
My best friend is dying. Ah, bittersweet.

      Never again to see longing in a man's eyes?
      What if I can't live with that?

Then, one May, a skinny Cherokee
scanned my curves and whistled.
A week later, we shared lunch.
He smelled like honey and incense
I've never felt old since.

True love—yeah, I can live with that.

See Sharp
(A Love Song in Two-Part Harmony)

<u>Soprano</u>

You were 21 years older, and
it took me a hundred scraped knees, knotted shoelaces,
and dripping Popsicles to catch up.

At first you were the melody,
leading the way,
providing my every smile.
We were bound together in a bright circle of song
while others watched silently, jealously.

You funneled sand from the hourglass of your mind into mine
one grain at a time.
I was your mirror image, following closely behind,
singing softly as I copied your rhythms, learned your notes.

Later, I ventured out of our circle,
made my own music,
though I still turned to you for approval, applause.

In time, we became equals.
I sang the melody in a clear, true voice.
You accompanied me on the piano
and sometimes joined in with two-part harmony.

Alto

Eventually, a cascade of false notes spun us apart,
Exploding our 21-year bond in discord.
Were we from the same phylum, let alone the same family?
Neither of us wanted to claim the other.
Our former intimacy became an uncomfortable secret,
best ignored.

Years passed. We remained out-of-tune strangers
sitting side by side at family reunions,
Two pretty heads turned away from each other in pictures.
Between reunions we strode purposefully
      in different directions,
trying to put as much space, time, and memories
      between us as possible.

Soprano

Now at life's sunset, I find myself using your expressions,
craving your derby pie, planting your daffodils,
reading The Decameron you kept by your bed,
imitating your tempos as I sing your songs.
Yearning to recapture the harmony.

       TANGLED THREADS

Twenty-one years apart in a lonely intermission,
but now at last, a reprise.
In my dream, you sit at the piano while I stand alone.
Cautiously we hum, then raise our voices in tendrils of song.
Avoiding each other's eyes, we grab each other with grace notes.

Just in time, we pull each other back to
See Sharp.
In tune at last,
we wrap each other
in a bittersweet duet of love and loss.

In the mirror above the piano, I see two tiny perennials,
tilled by life's cultivator, tempered by the furrows of seasons,
gray heads bending close together
creating the counterpoint of the mother-daughter refrain
as we share the music of our souls.

<u>Alto</u>

We have finally reached our crescendo,
found our perfect pitch and won our Grammy.
Thank God you melodied home to me.
No longer sad soloists,
we share a glorious generational madrigal.

Susan DeLay

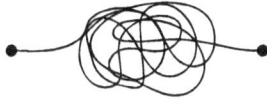

Writing Between the Lines

Susan DeLay puts pen to page,
A freelance writer at every stage.
Press releases. Ghostwritten books.
She polishes words and her readers are hooked.

Her blog, DeLayedReaction.com
Spins real life tales with wit and charm.
It's a mixture of humor, heart, and thought,
Sharing the lessons her life has taught.

Susan types fiction through sleepless nights,
Rewrites, reshapes, makes words tight.
Feedback fuels each new revision,
Her writers' group improves her vision.

Within history's echoes, she sharpens her pen,
Tackling truths from the now to the then.
Through pages she marches, no fact left alone,
Shaping lost voices to tales of her own.

In *Saving Jesus*, she bends time's thread,
Without a Prayer treads where Nazis led.
In *Without a Sound*, hands speak to save,
Then poetry called, so she's testing that wave.

A newbie poet, she always claims,
Oh, please, let's drop those reindeer games!
She rhymes like Dr. Seuss on speed,
Making up words when there's a need.

At fourteen, she started—a pro with a pen,
Reporting in Ohio, way back when.
Through publishing realms and columns well-spun,
She ditched Chicago for Florida's sun.

Honored to be with the First Friday crew,
She learns from them. They inspire her, too.
Susan's not legend. She's not a queen.
Just the snarkiest scribe that you've ever seen.

Ode to First Friday Soup

"Would you, could you give a thought
To joining my poetry group?"
Those words came from Pam, a poet of note
And the invite included some soup.

I thought poems required rhyme
So, intrigued and bemused, I said yes
Hoping to finally make sense of this world
And put my confusion to rest.

I admit, I've read couplets and dirges and odes
But never quite caught the drift
Of mathematical stylings with cadence and feet.
I just didn't have the gift.

So maybe amidst these women refined,
Who can't get enough of a sonnet,
I'd open my eyes to alliterative verse
And be able say, "Hey, I got it!"

I spent a whole week attempting a ballad
That would make Billy Collins so proud
But my hand at anaphoric repeat
I covered up with a shroud.

I tried lyrics and dirges and double dactyl
Elegies, limericks, and rhyme
But my Vorpal sword left me in uffish thought
And I was soon out of time.

I smelled the aroma of First Friday soup
As the deadline drew closer and closer.
The nearer noon came to my panicky brain
The more I thought, "Well, this is over."

Mere hours from taking defeat on the chin,
I faced my poetic crisis
And tackled the only solution I knew—
A doggerel of poetic license.

I scribbled an ode to a vegetable
It's one that I really hate.
Cooked carrots plus cadence and I was on board
Using quatrains and rhythm as bait.

Far from pastoral and further from epic
I hammered out rhyme after rhyme.
I passed haiku on the fast lane of meter
And raced to ye olde finish line.

Pam may be sorry she welcomed me in.
To turn my pentameter loose.
But time and time alone will tell
If I'm the next Dr. Seuss.

Nana Was Here

I learned all my letters when I was just four.
My As, my Bs and my Cs.
I mastered each one with a bright red crayon.
My favorites were A, N, and V.

I loved the letters that rose in sharp points
And longed to use them in words.
I grouped them together in NANA and VAN.
I know, I know. I'm a nerd.

Exhausting my paper and Ruby Crayola,
Which I'd worn down to a stub,
I went in search of a much bigger canvas
To show off my newfound word club.

I strolled past the bedroom of Daddy and Mom
And paused at the door of their room.
What's this? I thought as I spied a blank wall.
It's perfect for me and my plume!

I found a lipstick secured in a tube
And set out to work on my mural.
I wrote NANA in letters both tiny and large.
And sometimes I wrote it in plural.

I stepped back to admire my colorful work,
Pleased as could be with my art.
My future with words shone brightly ahead,
Or at least it was off to a start.

Wouldn't my parents be proud of their girl?
An original piece on their wall?
I could only imagine how thrilled they would be
Until I heard Mom's shrill call.

"Susan?" "Susan!" Her voice rang out,
Gaining volume with each command.
"Get in here," she cried in a very harsh voice.
Hmmm. I sensed reprimand.

As I stood before her, breaking out in a sweat
She pointed at her bedroom wall.
"Who did this?" she questioned, one hand on her hip.
I shifted my weight and I stalled.

Was there a chance she didn't know
Who'd created this art masterpiece?
My face as red as her Max Factor lips,
I asked, "Nana?" as my forehead creased.

As if my grandma'd swooped into their room
And unpacked her artistic pail.
I held my breath as Mom pursed her lips.
I knew then my answer had failed.

"Young, lady, just wait 'til your father gets home."
Famous words that always stung.
"Go sit in the chair that faces the wall.
And you think about what you have done."

I squirmed in our household naughty chair
And thought of my lovely creation.
Someday people will pay for my words.
This was part of my education.

My Dad tried to scold me, but couldn't disguise
The smile that broke out on his face
Especially when I tried to blame my Nana
For the art that had clearly defaced.

"Dad, I'm a writer! And someday you'll see
My words will go into a book!"
He nodded and said, "We shall see, Susie Q."
But by then, my goose had been cooked.

The Battle Over Cooked Carrots

The carrots stare up from the white Corelle plate
Rejected, unwanted, alone.
The potato, the roll and the chicken are gone.
Well, except for the chicken's wishbone.

The kitchen is clean and the food stowed away
In old recycled Cool Whip containers.
The dog licked up every crumb from the floor
And walked away at the speed of a glacier.

Our rule is to try everything on our plates.
One taste is all Mom requires.
But I'm not a good girl—at least not today.
Boiled carrots aren't what I desire.

Dessert is denied me because I've rebelled.
I have no choice but to comply.
Sit in my chair 'til the carrots are gone.
Sorry, but I'd rather die.

I hate Bugs Bunny's favorite dish,
Although hate's not a strong enough word.
They're awful when served up all buttered and hot
But worse as a clump of orange curd.

Dessert left the table an hour ago.
My brother and sister long gone.
They're watching "The Munsters" in stark black and white
While I sit in the kitchen 'til dawn.

I cross my arms and push back from the table
With resolve of a girl who is ten
When I spy our sweet Spaniel return to the room
Oh where, oh where has she been?

My heart leaps as in walks my foolproof escape—
A solution to leaving this prison.
For I am forbidden to vacate the place
Until I've devoured orange poison.

Surely my spaniel will help me escape!
She eats all that is tossed on the floor
From burgers to candy to frozen red grapes.
Will she eat cooked carrots? Beg for more?

I lure her with sweet words and hold out a spoon
Filled with the yucky gross mush.
Please puppy, eat up! There's as much as you want.
Just eat it and don't make a fuss!

I hold my breath as she sniffs at my spoon.
She pulls a bite onto the floor.
She rolls it around like a small doggy toy
Then backs away like she's bored.

No! No! Please come back!
I need you to stay!
Just swallow the carrots
And then go away.

She ignores me and ambles away from my sight,
Turning floppy deaf ears on my plight
I scoop the carrots back onto my plate.
I'm afraid that I'll be here all night.

At quarter past nine, Dad comes into the room.
He peruses my plate; says, "You're done.
Put your dish in the sink and head off to bed."

In the Battle of Carrots, I won.

The Day Frank Quit the Team

Grandfather Frank died when I was just ten,
And he was an old 85.
A retired judge with thinning white hair
He smelled of Chiclets, cherries and chives.

Son of a blacksmith in a one-horse town,
Population two-thousand eight,
Frank moved to Columbus to pursue a degree
At *The* Ohio State.

The DeLays were a smart and accomplished lot
Driven, loyal, energetic.
Devoted to family and God and the arts,
But athletic prowess? Pathetic!

So color his homies with shock and surprise
When Frank wrote to tell all the guys
He now played center on the football team
An Official Ohio Buckeye!

With thin padding of wool to protect his bones
And a leather cap for his skull,
Frank snapped the pigskin to the QB each week.
On occasion he ran with the ball.

Concerned for his safety, his mom wrote a note
"This game is a dangerous sport.
If you fail to cease and desist from this play
We must withdraw our support.

You won't see a dime for room, board or books
You alone will pay for your studies.
Hang up your cleats and your jersey and such.
Break away from those rough football buddies."

"But, Mother, the gridiron's perfectly safe,"
Said Frank on the edge of his dreams.
"Come watch a game and see for yourself
How secure I am on this team!"

Mom took a seat on the 40-yard line;
Her tight-lipped glare, far from subtle.
She watched her boy emerge from the scrum
For this was long before huddles.

Frank snapped the ball and the game was in play.
Then something went terribly wrong.
One of his teammates lay still on the field
Tackled by linemen so strong.

He didn't get up. Could not even try.
Fans and players held their breath.
Please be okay came silent prayers
But the player had met with his death.

A few days later, Frank got a letter
From his mother, Irene.
You probably already know what she said,
"Frank, you *will* quit the team."

In light of the death, he wasn't surprised.
His time on the field reached its end.
He chose law over football, a wise move, indeed.
His career as a jock? Pure dead end.

Frank traded his helmet for a Smith typewriter
And joined the student newspaper.
He toiled as a journalist, sharing the news
And as such, he found lots of favor.

But weekends found him cheering his Bucks
From a primo seat in the bleachers.
He never gave up on his love for the game.
Despite a career in legal procedure.

He passed in 1964
Leaving the world much brighter.
He bequeathed season tickets to his son, Tom
And I got his vintage typewriter.

A Great Man with an Early Tee Time

In memory of Tom DeLay (1923-2012)
A friend, a judge, a golfer, my Dad

What makes a man truly great, I ask?
Not just in words, but in actions that last.
Dictionaries may lack the right word or phrase
But my dad's life shined in countless ways.

In 2012, when he passed away,
I crafted his obit with dates and with names.
Since AP style frowns upon jest,
I followed the guidelines, though under impressed.

The finished piece was somber and boring
Leaving readers sad—close to snoring.
I believe obits should be half as fun,
As the person whose life is finally done.

So now I've a chance to fully share
A heartfelt tribute, if I dare.
Indulge me, my friends, as I proceed,
To say good-bye to a man of good deeds.

Dad had his passions, so many to name,
Coffee and Golf and Ohio State games.
Did I mention golf? Oh, what a thrill,
Gift shopping was easy, with just that one skill.

Golf equipment, hats, shirts and tees,
All repeats, but certain to please.
Once, when I wrapped up a Mr. Coffee
He looked confused; the gift wasn't golf-y.

"Why replace my old friend," he asked.
"When my ancient Bunn is still up to the task?
So I upped my game with a perfect gift.
A Dorf on Golf video, to offer a lift.

When his Bunn coffee maker "ground" to a halt,
I gave him a Keurig and he still found fault.
Greatness plus frugality, it's very true,
Especially when it came to his brew.

At the funeral home, tales came to light
Of mishaps and moments, long hidden from sight.
Hundreds lined up to pay their respects,
To hug us and cry, and also reflect.

When a woman was killed leaving four kids alone,
He considered adopting, expanding our home.
But fate intervened, distant kin was found,
No extra siblings on our school's playground.

A friend confessed, with a guilty grin,
He beaned my dad with a golf ball's spin.
But instead of anger, Dad gave a high five
As a compliment on the guy's lucky drive.

Dad's kindness extended, a heartfelt trait,
Even if the golf course had to wait.
He listened and cared, no matter the plea,
A politician with heart. Now, that's rare to see.

So, what defines a man as great?
Not riches amassed, or his fashion state,
Not diplomas hanging on the wall,
Nor fame nor touchdowns, big or small.

Greatness is found in laughter and grace,
In knowing oneself, with a smiling face.
In kindness that outshines personal gain,
In caring for others, through joy or through pain.

In the pre-dawn hours on a late July day,
He looked at my mom, gave a final wave.
He climbed aboard the celestial van
That took him off to Heaven's land.

I'm sure Dad had a tee time,
Arranged as a favor
With Payne Stewart, Ben Hogan,
And Jesus, his Savior.

Jen Haus

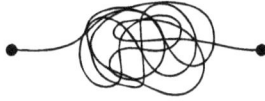

Jen Haus has been writing stories, poems and journal entries since she was a young girl when a family member gifted her a cornflower blue diary. That little book, over 40 years old, became the first of many journals in her ongoing love affair with pen and paper.

Jen's interest in creative arts and healing arts led her to pursue a bachelor's degree in English from Hofstra University as well as a Master's degree in Social Work from New York University.

After spending most of her adult life in NYC, Jen's life changed drastically several years ago, when life's circumstances brought her to live in The Villages to care for her mother. Going through major changes and losses, Jen was able to rekindle her creative spark and connect to amazing artists and writers in her new life.

The poetry she has shared in this collection focuses on the journey of witnessing her mother's struggle with dementia. Jen is so grateful to the poets in the First Friday Poetry Group who have given wonderful feedback and support. In addition to writing poetry, Jen is working on a memoir about surviving cancer two times.

Change of Seasons

Let go, move on, breathe.
watch the orange caterpillar inch over the Oleander branch
see how the golden sunlight slips into long shadows.

Let go, move on, breathe.
watch white clouds billow slowly across cobalt sky
see how the sky shifts from moment to moment.

Let go, move on, breathe.
watch the old woman gather dead leaves of better days
see how slowly she shuffles across the green grass.

Let go, move on, breathe.
watch lazy lizards soak up the steamy remains of the day
see the night gather and swallow her creatures.

Villanelle from Hell

My mother has lost her mind,
she asks me where it went.
She apologizes for not remembering.

What day is today, she asks me again,
why can't I remember anything?
My mother has lost her mind.

Outside the Oleander blooms pink,
orange caterpillars threaten the bark.
My mother apologizes for not remembering.

She asks me again, where I am going,
I want to crawl out of my skin.
My mother has lost her mind.

A palm tree sways stark against
cobalt sky and brilliant sunshine,
My mother apologizes for not remembering.

I remind her I love her.
She asks me why.
I repeat it again, then start to cry,
My mother has lost her mind.

The Boogeyman

I do not fear the Boogeyman
who looms inside her mind
where murky memory hides in the shadows.

The Boogeyman lives in her brain
evil creature from childhood
I do not fear the Boogeyman.

Details from her younger days
surrender to the monster
while dark veils dance in the shadows.

The Boogeyman fills her with fear
paranoid projections play out.
I do not fear the Boogeyman.

Doom and gloom compete while
cobwebs tangle in terror
her memory surrounds to shadows.

The Boogeyman is here then there
stealing her grip with sanity,
while I witness the madness.
Maybe I do fear her Boogeyman.

The Softening

Within these weeks, her memory fades
as the simple act of knowing time
becomes difficult and daunting.

Within these days, my heart breaks
as the intelligent, articulate Madonna
becomes a stranger to herself.

Within these hours, her being changes,
as childlike laughter then silly tantrums
become reminders for acceptance.

Within these moments, my love aches
as she apologizes with guilt
becoming maternal with realizations.

Within these times, my mother fades
as the daughter, oft impatient
becomes a gentler version of herself.

Deborah Hoffman

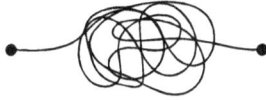

D eborah Hoffman taught literature and writing to smart students at the Alabama School of Math and Science, a state-sponsored boarding school. She is currently retired and is "practicing what she preached," through constructing her own stories and poems. She finds creativity a rewarding pursuit.

Parents

I wouldn't hug him
my father always
sheltering his tools
in the cellar his radio
talking

baseball players scoring
runs, landslides, storms,
houses burnt. People pay
with their lives my mother
never considered

a man running from
a woman always taking
what wasn't hers. Look at
her sister so much prettier
a showstopper

my curls curtailed
smiles shorn
still white anklets. My mother
kept her own wine corked
my mouth bitter

my father would leave me
hide if things got testy
I could dig myself out
or believe she was made
better than me.

Guardians

Guarding our garden
fencing barbed wired
tight as teeth.

My father shirtless
caresses fresh flesh
fat peaches blushing

bruised to the kitchen
he comes wishing a kiss
a sweetheart smile.

My mother reviles him
long legs reversing
straight as knives.

No earth clings as one
skirts the other.
They cannot help who they are.

My father crawling homeward
his mouth hot
fists curled into snails.

Love dries thin
as a dress
worn ragged.

If love is grief
I see myself loosen her
sour string of buttons.

If love is patient
I could catch him
at the border.

Kasiet

"There is only one religion and it is ecology."
Choltonbaev

Look there on the lone ridge of mountain
the flapping of a wing,
tall trees twist downhill
where bullrushes spell out the seasons.
Eager waves slap the shore.

Clutches of mourners come at sunrise
to drink the steaming waters of the springs,
to wash clean their sorrows.
A toil of generations
casting doubts, grievances
sprouting a sharp cry of prayer.

Each pilgrim leaves memories,
a token, a high note of hope.
So many knelt here before us,
readers of earth and sky,
bowing to each day of days.

We ask for the words
to praise our lives.

Look there where bullrushes
spell out the seasons.
No one kneels at the slapping waters,
bottled up for tourists,
their sandals scuffing
bare patches of soil.
Nothing catches hold.
A brambled path to the lake
loses appeal. The miracle gone.
Farmers flood the fields for food.
A pilgrim takes no comfort
as the sun ripens,
the wind drifts off course,
a whisper of feathers.

We leave no footsteps.

Sizing

We size each other up
weighing our differences.
I am keeping
my eye on you
who stay stationary
growing a bit with age
widening your girth.
You can be clumsy
but I'm even handed.
Serving you choice treats
gives me that whisper of control
as a woman.

Although when a man seizes
that watery shell
asks about age
state of health
and flips you upside down,
your outer parts
four legs suck in
head tucks sideways,
you have no voice.

Life is slippery
each lonely misstep measures
whether we are worthy.
Truth is how he holds you.

Dogfight

My dog is me
begging to be kissed
and hugged as a child.
Some parents dream to rough you up
stiffen your collar.
You fight to feel
who you are.

If folks take you for a ride
you can't stay in neutral.
Keep watch how they feed
or offer shelter.
People will always be
dangerous.

An old dog learns to protect
itself. Life whines down.
No matter how you worked
things out as a pup
you might not be able
to save us.

Dogs whimper alone in sleep.
Pretty bunnies nibble
the imagination. Tugging back
on the leash leaves me
breathless though to let go
even the best of us
discovers something to kill.

Arletia Mayfield

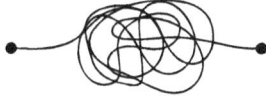

A rletia Mayfield is an ordained minister and the founder of The Prophetic Scribe Ministries & Publications. She offers courses and resources to help Christian writers and artists use their gifts in ministry. Arletia expresses her faith creatively through books, poetry, storytelling, skits, and worship with flags.

To learn more about Arletia Mayfield and The Prophetic Scribe Ministries, visit: thepropheticscribe.org.

His Voice

His voice reverberates
like an echo in my soul.
Demanding an audience.
A familiar voice.
Devoid of sound, yet,
He speaks loudly
to my mind, heart, and spirit.
Dictating plans
for my life.
I am His sheep.
I know His voice.
He says, Write the vision.
I am a ready writer,
poised to speak the words
of the one who knows
my past, present and future
in a glance.
My tongue fails.
Images form in the eyes of my understanding.
My pen moves swiftly across lined paper.
Capturing the words and pictures in ink.
Now, it's real.
A plan, a blueprint, a path,
orchestrated by the great I AM.
I know where I'm going.
His voice directs me onward.

Preacher Man

Preacher Man spoke from the pulpit.
The congregation was mesmerized.
They eagerly listened.

Preacher Man preached to his family,
The fear of God was the theme.
They pretended to listen.

Preacher Man stood on a corner.
Preached the gospel to the neighborhood.
No one listened.

Predators exploited the community.
Planned to conquer and expand.
They listened.

They decided Preacher Man had to go.
Warned him to stop preaching.
But he didn't listen.

They carried out their plan.
Left Preacher Man dying in the street.
Then everyone wanted the story.
Everyone listened.

The Rest Stop

In the warm embrace of a fleece robe.
I find a temporary substitute for his arms.

Sipping hot chocolate.
Whipped cream tickles my nose.

It's cold and wet outside.
Rhythmic drops plummet the motorhome roof.

Legs tucked beneath grandma's quilt.
Toes waltzing to nature's tune.

There's cocoa sediment in the bottom of my cup.
Why is the last sip the best?

Hearing the constant hum of engines.
Weary travelers preparing to rest for the night.

We all anticipate the next place.
Wherever that may be.

My husband is exhausted from driving hundreds of miles.
Running a business from the road is not easy.

When we stop and park, he doesn't stop.
There are calls to make, work to finish and deals to close.

Finally, my beloved crawls into bed.
His warm embrace replaces my fleece robe.

Raindrops, now a raging storm.
The sound of humming engines fades.

We snuggle and drift into blissful sleep.
Our dreams sailing oceans of expectation.

The Victim

I hid in the bushes
And peered through the trees.
At the sound of his voice
I dropped to my knees.
Didn't the passers-by even care.
Didn't they wonder why I was there?
I reach out for help and receive rejection.
Is being a victim such a nasty infection?

This Is Not My Home

In a realm not mine, I find my abode.
Unlearned about how to navigate this road.
My identity veiled in a mystery so deep,
My soul was stirred and compelled to seek.

In my quest for understanding, my heart did yearn.
I sought love in shadows where lessons were learned.
Addiction to pleasure was a perilous maze.
Intoxication held me captive in a haze.

In spirits distilled seeking solace and peace.
In the dance of desires my passions unleashed.
A hunger within, relentlessly swirled,
Until I became one of many lost girls.

Read the sacred text! God's voice to my spirit.
Wisdom is yours, so please don't fear it.
Your life, purpose, and destiny are clear.
Read these testaments! All the answers are here.

Discovering His origins, identity, and love.
Mysteries unfold about the Most High above.
Leading this seeker beyond the veil.
Where rewards await those who travail.

His kingdom, a refuge for the wandering and lost.
Admission is free because He paid the cost.
Entering through surrender, and faith by choice,
Opened my ears to hear his voice.

A sojourner through this place called Earth.
The only home I've known since birth.
This temporal place is a transient dome.
Incomparable to my eternal home.

Now, solace is found in an intimate place,
Where the Word of God is a warm embrace.
The dance of desire transformed into praise.
Living free, no longer enslaved.

Wisdom, knowledge, and understanding revealed.
Fate, identity, and destiny sealed.
Moving in wisdom not commonly known.
Keenly aware, this is not my home.

Pam O'Brien

Pam O'Brien began writing poetry at Allegheny College with a response to the Beatles' song "Strawberry Fields Forever," something we probably shouldn't try to respond to. A former resident of Buffalo, Erie and Pittsburgh, she worked in the fields of writing grants, teaching Spanish and English and teaching Professional Writing at the University of Pittsburgh for 19 years. Six years ago, she retired as a Professor Emerita to Florida.

In her new, warmer home, she volunteers at a local library and the VA, loves yoga and water aerobics and continues to write.

She has four chapbooks and two full-length poetry collections and has been frequently published in poetry magazines and journals. The most recent full-length collection, *Genealogy*, is a telling of family stories. During Covid, she wrote a novella and hopes to publish it someday. Part of her Florida experience has involved starting First Fridays, the women's poetry workshop that has put together this anthology.

She has three children (Boston, Pittsburgh and LA), three grandchildren and a mighty fine husband who also writes.

Why I Garden

Memory lives in a place that looks
like my perennial garden.
She wears Turk's Cap lilies and shadows.
She plays in the waterfall, pitches
pebbles, watches drops fall through
her fingers. She understands we live in now,
this moment. Yet her name
is Memory.

I dig in dirt and she buzzes snapshots
my father grilling hot dogs
my grandmother knitting fisherman sweaters
my daughter painting a neon green plaster kitten
my husband mumbling in his sleep

my tears as I climb off a plane in Madrid
my tears as I hold my first grandchild
my tears watering all those gardens in all those places.

This is Memory's workplace.
My work is to notice.

Gathering

Just when I think I've already lived
the happiest day of my life
along comes another surprise
from the universe

like last month when all three grown children
and their spouses and their children
came home for Christmas week.

They wanted to come.
They didn't fight.
Instead they played Clue
and went to church
and helped cook
and loved their ties and books
and carved wooden statues
we brought from Jerusalem.

The last night of all of us together
I watched the fireplace light washing
the walls. Even though it was winter
that room was again in full bloom.

I didn't think about losing
them back to their own busy lives.
I didn't mention that when
I look at them
I still see them
in their footed pjs.

The hustler winter moon
lurked right outside the window

but that night I was watching
the Chinese lanterns
glowing
flying
like silk on the nighttime deck.

Mothering

Molly is my dangerous child
the one who wandered away at amusement parks
took up risky competitions like high diving
and now the Transpac sailing race,
alone from San Francisco to Honolulu.

I imagined I wore my mother costume well with her
in spite of how it changed my college-girl body,
those leaking breasts, those puffy thighs,
that hip that never worked well again
after she bounced on it for two years,
and all that blood that came slipping
into the world she slid into.

Perhaps I never quite grasped losing
the woman I thought I would be
in exchange for being her mom.

Yet when she calls,
I still go running
on these tottering old limbs,
asking in a faltering voice
what can I do?
what do you need?
hoping that what she still needs is me
in spite of all I did to set her free.

Did my mother feel this same way
and I just didn't see it?
Did she understand
that along with the children comes
the sure knowledge that we secretly plan
to keep them, grip them, consume them,
that no matter who they are, like wolves,
we will raise them as our own.

How to Heal Yourself

Maggie, we are living in hard times.
Being a teenager, being scared,
being alone makes being hard.
You are the artist granddaughter.
and art is blessing and curse for sure.

I offer you this.

Find what it is that will feed your soul
      a book about Gothic architecture
      a walk to the reservoir
      a picnic in your backyard with the dog
      a small dinner of tomato soup, grilled cheese.

Understand that this won't be
your only time of despair.
Life is up and then down,
rarely balanced for long.

Do things to take your mind off loneliness.
Do what you can to help someone else
so the next time dark descends
when you lose someone you love
or get sick
or can't find the path
you will be more ready.

Learn how to stop, to rest.
Most of us spend a lifetime
figuring that one out.

And as you go on,
because I know you will go on,
keep writing, keep painting,
keep going back over all of it.

Each time it will be new again.

The Plan

"Tell me what it is you plan to do
with your one wild and precious life."
Mary Oliver

In this stage closer to death than birth,
I pace in a primitive hunger
to hunt, not relationships, but memories
to gather, not possessions, but words.

I remember
the house sparkling, the roast in the oven,
the children shaking snow from their coats,
the candles lit.
On my last day
I want to feast on that day.

I want to be completely used up when I go.
I want to have done more than I thought I could
       laughed more
       cried more
       ached more
       relished more
       worked harder
       played harder.

I don't want a tender, sweet body at the end.
I want to creak and groan and remember
      every bike ride
      every hike
      every bouncing horse
      every roller coaster

      every baby whooshing from my body
      every grandchild snugging on my lap

      every single night of sweet, hot love.

Most of all, I want to have said
what I came here to say
that this dear life was worth it
that my faith tells me this is not the end
that my God has been and will always be there.

I want to have no words left.

Bonnie Pearson

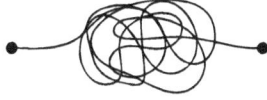

Bonnie Pearson, a retired corporate writer, earned degrees in psychology and literature in her home state of Pennsylvania. A Floridian for the past 25 years, she enjoys extensive travel with her husband and has visited more than 180 countries. Africa is her favorite destination, especially since she and her spouse were married in Tanzania in a tribal ceremony carrying baby goats.

In addition to travel, she enjoys making soup for sick people and reading voraciously. She takes great pride in her vast collection of table runners. To ward off the ravages of aging, Bonnie works out at the gym and pool.

She wishes she had a Golden Retriever.

Choices

You take what you want from life
then you pay for it.

Child or no child?
Patent leather Mary Janes
or traveling the world?
Plump petal lips—would she look like me?

Did I want the Arctic, China, Peru
or screeches that scissor the ear?
Neediness and endless questions?
Tempers that scorch the soul?

Or a little girl curled in my lap
as she learns to love *The Velveteen Rabbit*
witnessing a mind and heart develop
and those little socks with ruffles on the cuffs?

Chaos vs. Krakow
Boredom vs. Borneo
Tantrums vs. Tibet
Diapers or Dalmatia?

Having adventures triumphed over
civilizing a self-focused little being
Reading books, watching movies geared to me
trumped Three Little Pigs and Snow White

Fussing or Figi
I made the right choice.
Giving up giant grosgrain bows
to get a life totally mine, but

I would have called her Skyler.

Adoration

The priest lifts the sacred host,
surrounded by golden beams,
his silver-embossed stole flashing in the candlelight,
the pure white host, the magnitude of God in a tiny circle.

The bells ring, wafts of incense fill my nine-year-old head,
profound awe,
innocent infusion of pure light,
God—right there before me.

A hymn—"Sweet Sacrament We Thee Adore,"
and I did! I did!

Decades later and now more free,
the Spirit of Life still awakens adoration,
growing more brilliant daily,
the Source fills me with crystalline air.

That fountain of joy infuses each cell with happiness,
a broader focus,
a desire to be blessed by its flowing waters,
the bliss—oh, the bliss.

No bells or whistles needed.

Sea Bliss Sonnet

The water ripples with my thoughts,
my peace settles and anchors in its depths,
my joy sparks and flashes on its surface,
a flying fish arcs.

The puffball clouds delight,
the wind teases my hair from its combs
my Nordic beloved's arm around my waist
and the air—the sweet and perfect air

kisses my lungs.
The foam is the sea's laughter,
the sky her Easter bonnet,
her jewels lie scattered in the seaweed.

This is where I sail heaven.
This is where I should be.

Astonished

I forget that I'm old
as I gallop headlong into
the middle of my mid-seventies.
I forget that the word "elderly" applies to me.

But sometimes, I'm reminded
as a perfectly linear crop of gray hairs
sprout up a full moon after my last coloring
and won't be hidden by a clever part.

The message comes through
when a reflected image in the microwave door
is wrinkle-ravaged and I gasp,
"Who can she be?"

And my joints remind me too
when little sharp daggers puncture hips and hands.
Whose pain can this be?
Certainly not the owner of these supple bones.

But most of the time, I'm 54,
tumbling like a waterfall singing in its descent
into full-tilt joyous living.
And I'm astonished—"How can I be almost 75?"

Ten Pots

Ten flower pots sitting a row.
The first holds ruffled blooms of glory.
The plants diminish as one looks down the row,
through dwindling stages of loveliness.

A new bloom enters,
resplendent in riotous color,
so the last plant must go,
no longer worthy of a place in line.

Life mimics the row in continual balance,
old outfits give way to new closet entries.
A holiday table runner that once gladdened the heart,
surrenders to a crystal globe that currently brings joy.

Unread books line up in order—
how lusciously they fill sweet times of leisure.
A new masterpiece demands to be read,
the maybe-someday book exits the line.

Friends who once brought joy but do so no longer,
now move down the row,
as new folks enter with their fresh light,
and some, oh-so-precious ones,
never yield their spot.

A line of pots—the river of living,
flowing in—flowing out,
balance and bliss.
The tenth pot yields.

Helcha

Her apron smelled of bleach on Mondays
and lilies of the valley the rest of the week.
She was short and round—the child of immigrants.
She sang me lullabies in Polish.

She said "haitch" instead of "aitch,"
was somewhat controlling,
not as American as I,
such tiny faults in one so kind.

She sewed me doll clothes—knitted me an afghan,
sacrificed for private schools.
She ironed my uniform blouses,
made me a doll cake with a ruffled icing skirt.

I could have been so much nicer to her
but my pseudo-sophistication blocked my gratitude
She earned nicer than I gave—
teen contempt and haughtiness.

She died at 62 when I was 30
not yet grown into my kinder, wiser self.
So many questions left unanswered
because I did not know enough to ask.

Now a hole replaces the answers I do not have.
What were her dreams both dashed and realized?
Did her years in the convent change her soul?
How do you crochet?

Kay Rawls

Kay was 20 before she realized she could write poems and essays. While working on her under-graduate degree in English and Math, the Southern Literary Festival in Waco, Texas, named her runner up in their poetry category.

Two years later, in 1962, Kay began teaching high school English and Math. During those years, she completed her Master's degree in Psychology as well as certification as a school psychologist. She worked as a school psychologist in the Metro Nashville Public Schools for fifteen years.

During that time, Kay and a close friend tried writing song lyrics, hoping to sell something to well-known singers in Music City. She had no musical background and, she claims, no talent.

In 2003, Kay and her husband Jim retired and moved to central Florida. In 2005, Kay joined a poetry website and dove back in to writing poetry. Scores of poems later, she tried her hand at prose. Eight to ten short stories later, she tried a novel.

A decade or so later, Kay took a hard look at her lack of success as a poet/writer and sadly concluded that she was the only one who believed she had the talent and skills to write professionally. And on a particularly dark afternoon in late May, she destroyed all copies of 300 or so of her poems and a handful of her short stories. From that day on, she has written only a handful of poems and these, prompted by some noteworthy social or political event that moved her spirit to reply.

Lines

In reply to Wordsworth's
"Lines Written Above Tintern Abbey"

A score of winters now has passed, yet not
In twenty has there been snowstorm so fierce,
So wild as this, where every living thing,
As in the Flood, is hidden from the sky,
Oblivion's large, cold, broken hands to feel.

A long, bare, tedious winter stayed the snows
On jagged mountain cliffs and sunken vales
Until benevolent Nature winged her way
Once more, a dove in search of fig leaves scarce.
As ore the glittering, colorless landscape
She sped, arousing silent, sleeping snows
And caused them ere a month or more to flee
On downward paths and offer drink, as alms,
To lands below who stood athirst and begged
For half a sustenance from thy deep well.
Yet more those crystal rivulets did send
Than worthy humble praise of earth to me;
They sent a poet's spirit ever there.

Now earth once more a temporal purity knows
Because thou once beneath dark sycamore
Did lie and reminisce of countryside,
Of chilly mountain streams and of thy youth;
'Cause thou alone of thine own age failed not
To hope that kindness would outlive the man.

The Edge of Mercy

"There's a wideness in God's mercy,
Like the wideness of the sea ..."*

I have seen the sea from both sides,
walked barefoot each furlong of its fence row
that my own eyes might know
the length and breadth of it
taking no one else's word for just how wide it is.

I've seen the frayed edges of it
where it slammed through centuries
against steep unforgiving cliffs
and where it washed against same centuries

of sand but was unwelcome when
but hours had passed and
tide had turned.

I know, then.
that there are places
the sea cannot go.

Where, then, cries my soul,
are the places
mercy cannot go?

Where are the edges
where it begins to fray

and unravel?

How tall are the cliffs
it cannot scale?

How wide is the wideness
of the sea?

*Lyrics by Frederick W. Faber, Oratory Hymns, 1854

Slumber Party

Alone,
unseen, unfed, unbathed,
crouched in the corner of her grief,
blinds drawn against the light,
mindless of the cold
they kept inside

Her friends found her there at noon.
(The four E's, she called them)
Born of the same muse,
inseparable by the years between them,
they came to save her.

Emily, kneeling close beside her,
caressing her tangled hair,
offering great wads of Kleenex,
cooing, "It's OK, we're here now."

Erica, cursing the absent one,
ranting and screaming, "The bastard!
I'll kill the son of a bitch myself!"
(She was the mean one in the bunch.)

Edna, rubbing her cold feet,
offering a warm blanket,
knowing that this was not a case of
"broke my heart in little ways."

Elizabeth, the mathematician of the lot,
knowing the heights and breadths
a heart could reach; struck dumb
by the depths and widths.

Knowing that the chasm of her bed
would swallow her alone,
they tucked her in with gentle hands
and slipped in next to her.

Three days and two nights
they stayed with her,
bringing her small bowlfuls of salvation,
feeding it to her in tiny spoonfuls,
hoping its warmth would reach her soul.

They spoke at first of familiar things:
the "first sweet pea" they picked today,
and "crazy salads" they had made,
not once chancing to say,
"You, me, we can be hurt that way."

They took turns reading aloud to her,
"All the little boats that ever sailed the sea,"
soft words in soft voices,
bandaid kisses
for a lethal wound.

On the third day
Sylvia came by
and made them all get out.

She would take over from here.

A Parable Retold

Tis not degree or length of flame
that doth a fire prove, but power
to lend its flame to waiting hearth
or slender taper still unlit
yet never suffer loss, as coin
would do, of lend.

Tis power to warm
the willing heart and light renew
in eyes long absent love's bright flame
yet suffer not the consequence
of strength subtracted from its own.

Tis power to multiply and give
again.

Tis fish and loaf of love.

Welcome, Then, the Loss

Tis not malfunction's rare mistake
nor dread deformity of birth
nor that it sudden cease to beat
the heart should deem as greatest threat.

The heart's real danger, I would learn,
lies not along its ragged edge
of random trial and error run,
nor in safe sand of childhood play
and bright pretend, nor in life's vow
consigned in fever to the page.
It frets in vain the false precept
of loss in such peripheral place
so far removed in circumstance
from love's white axis at its core.

Nor ever can the heart be rent
by purposeful design nor cut
with knife of calculated risk
but only severed from the self
in excruciating accident
of alchemy compounded in
the willing cup and drunk without
recourse or requisite relief
of strength or power certain stirred
or knowing then profound effect
of full its drinking would ensure.

But, oh, the savage sacrifice
of heart ne'er freely given to love.
Its lingering loss sits daily in
the absent chair at table spread
and mocks the place where it would eat
and leaves behind its clumsy shoes
to wait at doorstep ere it would
return in constant, cold remind.

Tis hour, then, that welcomes loss,
that stands at door thrown open wide
and urges in the prodigal one
and clasps the hand and kisses full
the face of long-awaited joy.

The Weightlessness of Matter

Your timidness tore at me,
Squeezed all the air from my lungs.
wrapped its fingers around my heart,
erasing decades that lay
in silent graves
between then and now.

But there we were
suddenly in fifth grade all over again
and you, eyes downcast,
walking down the empty hall
toward me, wanting to look up,
mind shut down in its search
for something memorable
to say.

And, mute with the same loss,
unable to retrieve all my
practiced witticisms,
my calculated cleverness,
myself at once poor
of words to spend.

The moment
fluttering on frail wings
between us,

our bodies weightless
as we passed.

Acknowledgements

The First Friday poets are firm believers in the fact that we do not write in a vacuum. We have helped and inspired each other in the creation of these poems.

Many thanks to Lorraine Benjamin for the cover design.

And many thanks to Jack O'Brien who said, "I think you should put your poems together in a book and I'll publish it."

Spicy West African Stew

Ingredients
1T oil

1 large sweet potato, peeled and diced

8C chicken broth

1/2t cumin

1t thyme

3C salsa

1C diced not peeled zucchini

1 large chopped onion

1C raw brown rice

2/3C peanut butter

3 cans garbanzo beans, drained

Making It
Saute the onion and sweet potato in oil,
until softened, about five minutes.
Add the broth, thyme, cumin and rice.
Once boiling, simmer for 20 minutes.
Add the salsa, zucchini and garbanzos.
Simmer for five minutes.
Add the peanut butter.

Invite your friends.

First Edition November 2025
ISBN: 9798990138513
Cover + interior design: Liliana Guia
Cover photo: Lorraine Benjamin

Published by Coursaire, LLC
The Villages, FL 32162 USA
permissions: capnjob@gmail.com

Printed in USA

www.ingramcontent.com/pod-product-compliance
Lightning Source LLC
Chambersburg PA
CBHW072356090426
42741CB00012B/3056